THE BOOK OF STONES AND ANGELS

HAROLD
SCHWEIZER

POEMS

# THE
# BOOK
# OF
# STONES
# AND
# ANGELS

T|P

Tupelo Press
North Adams, Massachusetts

Library of Congress Catalog-in-Publication
data available upon request.
[ISBN: 978-1-936797-63-9]

Cover and text designed by Josef Beery.
Cover: "Archaeopteryx lithographica (Eichstätter Specimen)"
Wikimedia
First paperback edition: October 2015.

Tupelo Press
P.O. Box 1767, North Adams, Massachusetts 01247
Telephone: (413) 664–9611
editor@tupelopress.org
www.tupelopress.org

Tupelo Press is an award-winning independent literary press that
publishes fine fiction, nonfiction, and poetry in books that are
a joy to hold as well as read. Tupelo Press is a registered 501(c)(3)
nonprofit organization, and we rely on public support to carry
out our mission of publishing extraordinary work that may be
outside the realm of the large commercial publishers. Financial
donations are welcome and are tax deductible.

*for Saundra Kay*

# Contents

*A stone cannot feel its falling.*

HENRI BERGSON

*I, Stone, fell into affliction*
*worse than*
*the annealing of glass through the whole series of endurable pains*

*and worse.*

ALICE OSWALD

# THE BOOK OF STONES AND ANGELS

## And We?

At the end of each day
a little time is left it
slows into a leaf a stone
a fountain a thing
is a trace of time

And we?

The same the things
we have held the rooms
we have lived in dream
us and angels

# Of Stones and Angels

*These stones to praise thee may not cease*
GEORGE HERBERT

The north wind had turned the underside of the
leaves up towards the sky then there were two days
when the air was still and all was clear and I
remembered how you would peel the peas how you
would touch and fluff the small frail leaves of the
spring salad
             I woke up at two and felt the night
move along my body at the speed of plant growth
and I lay still on my side breathing in the rhythm of
time passing over me like a loom and in its folds
time was darkest and it smoothed and lengthened
itself against my body and stretched and thinned
and became light
             late when the sun was setting and
the shadows lengthening across the river and the
fish leaping and the swallows fast dipping down to
the foil surface I slid upriver to the rock and was
turned by the current gentle as a mother and was
back as the light was waning and the groundhog
was grazing who did not hear my steps nor the
light still as glass nor the stars like stones under
water
             the sweet basil had grown
translucent roots frail as the fins of fish in the jar I
had watered I never spoke to it but it grew one

bitter word and it would have wilted I will never
see you sleep again

All night long I heard the whirring wheels of the
cicadas and the shriek of the night owl and the
intermittent mouthsounds of little animals and the
sudden flutter of songbirds I woke in the early
morning the air hovered on the pond and the trees
gathered and waited on the slope out my window
and the sun came red through the rising mist
                    then the days turned cooler and the
sun cast shadows of tree branches against the walls
the first frost killed the cicadas the summer sounds
were gone the nights were still the trees were
barren the river gently swept
                    I left no lights on outside set no table
did not stay awake to hear the door you did not
come home anymore I did not think I heard the
door I did not stay awake to hear the car I did not
lean on my arm did not see the night passing like
water over a bed of stones

Angels are invisible we move among them blindly
we see only things we force them to confess their
particularity to reveal their distinct outlines to
perform their faint flat emanations as if they had to
justify their capricious existence that is why stones
look opaque and mortified when we hold them in
our hands we sense their shyness that they will not

recover that they are only signs manifestations of
something beautiful and terrifying we drag them out
of their invisibility turn them in our hands look at a
stone's underside but only see its eerie specificity
its blandness of color its blunt shape we feel its
indefensible weight and doubt that it mirrors our
fortuitous existence that we share the ontology of
stones that we too are metamorphoses of angelic
movements movement turned to matter
                    they smell after they have been
handled and take years to settle back into their old
positions of enduring

An angel's wing lies fossilized in the cool shade of
its weight enduring the density of matter densest
where the joints grew into the shoulder and most
porous along the feathered edges where stones
retain their luminous angelic origins stones are
slow shy and awkward we doubt it and do not feel
the rush of light that comes off a stone but all
material things are remnants of visitations come
about through the bending and falling of time
between a wing and a joint
                    all are fragments of angelic
movements of unceasing arriving and departing
and we mistake them for stones houses bridges
fountains gates pitchers fruit-trees windows or
heard them when we were happy as birdsong or
they keep us awake at night do we not feel a breath

sit up eyes wide open arms outstretched thinking
we heard something but see only the night blunt as
stone and hear the house? do I not turn and
something moves and tears and I turn again
thinking I had seen a house a stone a roof
a garden?

Their descending and arising is only matter to us
they are only visible we only know them all around
us stones are increasing in density the earth nudges
them gentle as air lifting and shifting them
immeasurably in the rhythm of their original
eternity we cannot see it matter will not recover
stones will not rise up houses will not fly we will
remain among things for angels are only in the
endurance of things
                    but the sudden draft of light in the
upsweep of a wing is repeated in the water's slow
flowing and the numb stone's imperceptible lifting
and sinking

Then the sun came through the windows and the
walls tables and doors clarified and the yellow light
stayed and flowed and I did not know what to say
except for standing in the hall looking and looking
one hand on the chest of drawers as if to steady
myself just standing and looking and calling into
another room come look this light look how it fills
the room sweeps across the floor and flows against

the wall how it pools on the floor moves and
retreats no one answered the sun moved behind
the clouds

        I doubted the angels and their
vibrating geometric scaffolding in the sky


They lie in obscure spaces so that they do not feel
looked at but I can hear them and feel their
nocturnal destinations their continuous weight
their far unhurried displacements of air I keep
them from falling I lift them and carry them in my
sleep I brought a stone out of the night that had
been falling a large one grayish dull wet and tired
of its weight it had begun to split and I could reach
into its side and feel its slowness while it leaned
shyly against my hand recovering a little and I saw
how out of the porous edges of a stone a little light
flowed slow as a child's breath against a hand while
in the densest center where the joint fused with the
bone I felt the destiny of things their necessary
circumference and weight there a stone is heaviest
there it is most difficult to keep it from falling if it
falls it will fall with its center first

        meanwhile the sky was vast and
unbroken the windless air carrying the voices of
school children was clear and high and the stone
lingered in my hand it was not worth repairing
anymore

I had looked through them one by one each was
surrounded by silence each had fallen through the
shaft of its particular destiny to assume its weight
and shape and composition as if to deceive us of its
angelic origins but if we had let them be then on
rare occasions when we would not have been
waiting anymore we would have felt them press
against us gently by a force that we mistake for
falling or we would have felt their presence as a
humming or we would have felt a draft as if
somewhere a door had opened and someone
suddenly left

               and they might have leapt up faintly
as if they had enjoyed a sudden levity and they
would have ascended through the foliage of time
once more and we would have known that they
were there because they looked at us each with its
sheen from the north wind and each would have
been wholly attentive to our presence each in its
surprising singularity of shape density weight and
composition each as deep and incomparable as
an iris

               they would have known how each of
us had come to our bodies like them by falling that
we resembled them in our material composition
and in the density of our bodily center (which is the
fear of death) and they would have known us and
regarded us intimately and they would have seen us
and we would have felt their weight

               and the lightness of their gaze

Although everything has mass circumference and
weight and leans or lies against and darkens
something else although stones lie motionless in the
increments of light falling evenly as rain although
their materiality relieves them from all obligations
some stones recall their former shapes of sternum
clavicle scapula humerus

                    they are allegories of something
other than their mass they are not dense they are
concentrated as if they were thinking to be
something other than what we think they must be
they are not stones merely but *stones of* that which
once moved them and made them alight and
descend and which we having lifted a stone from its
oblivion and holding it all through the night

                    feel as a slight expiration that we
mistake for the pull of gravity nor is it our doubt
but their alienation that renders stones something
other than what they are despite their apparent
simplicity (some are bitter) they cannot cease from
pointing beyond their mass and weight which are
in proportion to their estrangement

A stone's speed is inconspicuous it lingers with a
slowness inconceivable to us it seems merely to lie
somewhere in what to us looks like the accident of
its falling but it waits yielding its side expecting to
be touched

those that remain untouched store
the grief of children while those few that we lift and
carry slightly expand and open themselves some
begin to split and some exuberantly break so that
we become the bearers of grief and we begin to
understand that a stone's mass and density are only
ways of keeping secrets some feel the vibrations of
machines and exude minuscule amounts of
moisture their thread-thin veins expose all that
hurts and cannot be mended

some places on our bodies are
superfluous there we have not been touched these
will turn to stone the breastbone feels like a shield
in the body the spine rises high above the back
the clavicles extend the force to move the wings

# Of the Limited Amount of Silence Light and Space

## I

It is bad to die without the silence of the grievers'
eyes their speechless presence their sheer giving of
themselves the disappearance of silence is the most
inconspicuous of all privations we do not even think
it happens nor do we miss it except at moments
when something we had hoped would still be
possible is found to be futile then our silence has
been taken and there is no space for us where we
can be alone

## II

Though the sun stands high in the southern arch of
its rising there is no light nor do we know there is
no light what we see is only what we have seen and
continue to see as if there were light and so the
darkness moves about us and we move within it

## III

Then space contracts to the dimensions of a small
backyard in a windless city then to a windowless
cell then to a closet then it swallows a last spindle
line of space as if an invisible ladder that had leaned
against the passage of time was no more

IV

Nor is there wind in a stone nor does a leaf fall in it
its innermost matter lies layered like a tightly folded
landscape if one were to unfold a stone one would
find in it thin as the pages of a book the remnants of
light and the hand that had opened the stone would
lie still like a hand that had marked a passage in a
book lightly with a faint pencil line

# Of Angels

*. . . es nähme / einer mich plötzlich ans Herz*
RAINER MARIA RILKE


Their eyes are long filaments of light the updraft of
it extinguishes the weight of machines ships houses
trees and stones they fly because they cannot fall
we cannot see it but every stone emits a little light
even in a stone's charged atomic nucleus where its
weight is heaviest where its mass is most intense
they rise and descend their eyes are open they
never close them for them all things are merely
delicate membranes
                they lift up with tiny leaps at
our approach and keep ahead of us repeating their
hesitant retreats
                once I thought of them
merely as movement better the more insubstantial
best as nothing but they are gentle as glass they
inhabit all things they are not particular they do not
prefer water to stone air to earth or flowers
because of their brevity
                when we look at them we
confuse their alignments they seem to turn away
from us and lie hunched in stones our eyes render
them incomplete we touch them but only feel a
scribble of minerals and metals we cannot open
them

they will not come out of
their habitations they have gone into the gloom of
matter

Although we always mistake them for their
appearances we intuit their dwelling in things when
we lift and set them down and the movements of
our hands continue in them and we sense duration
deep within what we thought was the inertia of
matter
                    and we feel that matter
moves and that stillness is a delicate continuity and
that time is as incomprehensible as their
inhabitation of things that we endure not only as
things but as presences of angels that all things
stones bridges fruit-trees gates windows are their
temporary occupations and that the only difference
between unfeeling matter and living things is our
feeling of being drawn into their gaze

The stones I gathered from the bottom of the river
are breaking in places small as hair
                    like a blind person who feels
a window I feel a fugue of light faint but
continuous like a draft of air I run my hands over
their surfaces I walk through the green light of fern
in the night the wind moves the branches in and
out of the sound of water I carry the stones in small
boxes and set them down with the lids ajar

And if they had no mass neither would they have
duration nor extension nor weight even light would
be a burden to them neither would their breath
have span nor would there be any interval between
the contractions of the beating wings nor for any
other reason than for the sake of things do they
encumber themselves with matter nor do they
have wings

## Of the Limited Amount of Hatred
## Apportioned to Each


Like love or hope but unlike the infinite half-life
of pain hatred is apportioned according to need

like a daily bowl of rice having been spent on hair
the weather a too tight-fitting lid a broken nail

eventually it becomes a scarcity we hate less or less
well until one day we run out of it entirely wholly

devoid of it mildly surprised by a sudden blankness
for example while the news reports of an endless

stream of refugees waiting in line on a long dusty
road prompting our wistful agreement that

somehow beyond one's always only local concepts of
justice they must have called it upon themselves had

they striven hard enough been more clever sorry
that history must be embodied by somebody else a

pleasing thought of gratitude occurs how much less
expensive the expansion of the sunroom had turned

out how rare when everything always costs more
the fees for golfing the use of the tennis courts

# Antoine Le Sauteur, Maître de Cave

*Note nécrologique sur Antoine Le Sauteur, 1925–1996.*
*Eloise, le 9 novembre 1996, est décédé Monsieur Antoine Le*
*Sauteur, Maître de Cave, Veuf de Clara, née de Clicquot . . .*
LE DAUPHINÉ LIBÉRÉ


Cellar-master Antoine Le Sauteur fell in the year of
his death down the staircase and cracked his head
open on the stone floor next to the riddling rack
                he felt the sharp of the stone's
infernal casting
                the angel came to lie in his
body effervescent as a flake of alabaster Antoine
cupped his hands over the place on his temple
where the angel had entered and found himself


In the insular stillness of his childhood
                I would have given her apple
blossoms (he said) and white moving clouds I would
have thought of a sudden clearing in the brown tree
light I would have made the sheep graze against the
distant sky voices waft from the pasture like pieces
of wind we would have picked small white and
yellow flowers and carried them in paper for a while


Lifting his head he brushed his hand against the temple
arm of his broken glasses on the stone floor
his head was opened he could hear its lisps of
valves and clefts its mass minutely swayed it frayed

and feathered in sudden wafts it loosed
a yellow leaf
        and Antoine Le Sauteur felt
in his head the uncoupling of the leaf from the twig
in the tiny tubular hollow of the leaf's stem in the
tug when it fell
        when it fell the angel's wing
like the pointer of a sundial lingered a moment and
cast a shadow


Then Antoine dreamt that angels rose from the
Rhône lifting their hunched weight like the heads of
bald old men stooped over some incomprehensible
underwater work both arms extended perhaps to lift
the riverbed perhaps to hold it down perhaps to
unbend a shaft of light
        he dreamt his wife Clara was
lying next to him in the damp undergrowth that she
too saw them opening the water with their long
invisible arms that she too heard them waking the
river's sleepers


Was she calling him Antoine Antoine where are
you what have you done she came down the cellar
steps her face
        of water and wind and
kneeled and held his head in her lap Antoine
        see the cuts and abrasions

where the angel turned and beat its wing against
your face how it must have flown high and fast
in the rafters of our house how in your head's
peripheral depression a little time has pooled
                    and stirring it with her
breath she revived


In him the clamor of night and rain the first days of
fall while the angels smoothed their vanes and barbs
and resumed their invisibilities in the claustrophobic
secrecy of things houses streets lights cars Clara was
a blank of darkness thrown on the curb dragged the
sudden weight of her up the staircase lay in the span
of their wing
                    stroke still and beating
without which nothing could endure so vast that we
mistake it for things—


And then Antoine knew that although the beating
of their wings engenders death angels don't know
what death is
                    for them it has the anatomy
of a stone for when Antoine looked up to rest
his gaze on Clara's face the angel looked back
at him from inconsolable matter then Antoine fell
from sleep to sleep hearing children's voices across
fields mown before sunrise his house drifted
through the night

and he heard the shadow of
Clara's breath when she slept in the shadow of his
breath he leaned on his arm and read


One hand on the edge of light the other in the
dream's pages he started to sing to her in a garden
of ancient trees whose branches spread the blades of
angels' wings

*They drive the sap green the leaves*
*bloom the chestnut light*
*the yews' green tips they leaf*
*the purple sage the fern and ivy*

*lean the mouths of lilies toward*
*the searing sun rise in the slow*
*growth of mountain laurel fly*
*in the silver lace vine's speed lie*
*down in the scent of lavender*
*and rosemary turn in the center*
*of a stone wind a path through*
*the gloom of tree-light mute*
*the sudden sky fold the mountains*
*and throw down deep valleys*


When they were young she had taken a metal bird
from a shelf in a house in the Lüneburger Heide she
had held it out to him across planes of light when
the bird was almost to leave her
                    hand she said she felt a
somnambular movement there was no world before
or after it other than that fluted in the angel she said
and dropped the bird
                  they did not know that the
angel had crossed over colorless siliceous sands
already bearing their sorrows in the rhythm
of its flight


Rain had fallen all night long hard into the woods
and the cut logs in the shade were moss-green soft
                and a thin line of light flew out
into the darkness (it was the third night)

After Clara died Antoine's life became a house full
of old and useless things glass bottle stoppers
children's crates an old garden gate an antique
wheelbarrow and country jars for growing flowers a
small wooden scooter two iron wheels from an old
perambulator and a candle stand with lighted
candles Clara
                        he called Clara are you not
wearied by the incessant draft can you feel
the terrible breach stand in the wind with me
the weather has turned blue and gray a shiny crust
of ice has formed on the edge of the wind is it
the wind that makes us weep


But the wind had ceased he had slept too long in the
river's weight he had dreamed in the river's arm he
could feel its silent grinding sheath


And the stones opened from deep within where a
stone's matter weeps densest gravity there a child
carried cornflowers yarrows and daisies from
somewhere as far away as water and Antoine knew
in its eddies the river remembers the limbs of the
drowned and in its flowing it forgets them and flows
                        and the angel folded the stone
until it was saturated with matter and it lay down in
the stone's weight

Now Antoine Le Sauteur Maître de Cave in the
small hamlet of Eloise he of the stone floor heard
Clara's voice singing far away

*we will walk again through ochre*
*fields and see the branches of tall*
*redwoods swinging in the wind*
*how the wind moves the branches*
*in and out of light and hear*
*the sound of water in the leaves*
*we will come to a still pool*
*where a green-breasted bird*
*alights mosquitoes flit like rain*
*water-striders shudder across*

*the glassy film we will say*
*we have walked through ochre fields*
*and heard the sway of long green waterweeds*


And Antoine tried to raise himself on his arm Clara
holding on to the riddling rack he cried Clara
Clara a house in green woods you opened the gate
only to say go I am not in danger how it came about
that I stopped and knew you had opened the gate


The grass blades trembled the flower stalks wilted and
turned brittle the river changed a tree leaned and fell
its top branches nodded and swept in the current drift-
wood trash and leaves caught in the branches soon
the drowned logs would lie in embraces of silt and clay
downstream from the fallen tree the Rhône flowed
combed in small rivulets and quieted

## Of the Limited Amount of Falling
## Apportioned to Each

I

They will find themselves suddenly weightless to
test their disbelief they will seek out staircases

open shafts precipices tall buildings they delicately
throw themselves into the air and awkwardly hang

there until someone helps them down the better
among them join airborne divisions rescue teams

balloonists window washers crane operators while
the worse enlist in the ranks of the proud the

committers of hubris when they try to fall asleep
they have to pull themselves down onto their beds

like divers buoyed by too much air all of them are
eventually overcome by a great fatigue for which

there is no remedy other than falling but they
cannot fall exhausted undeceived loveless well

and voluble they smile they wave they lean the
irretrievable weight of their bodies sharply forward
their hands grabbling the ground before them

## II

Few fall silent suddenly the loss of words happens
gradually it is not that one doesn't remember a word

it simply isn't there anymore it has been recalled to
an invisible repository out of which each of us was

once apportioned a share of *flower* of *find* of
*who* of *night* of *leaf* not all equally some of us run out
sooner

than others politicians street vendors teachers
mothers while the monosyllabic the shy

the taciturn have been endowed with a prophetic
sense that deep within their bodies their words are

numbered those they used prodigally like *like* and
*and* or *so* or *not* or *or* or *I* one day no longer come to

their lips then briefly they will say *oh sorrow*
*house* they have to proclaim their love by leaving
the bud of a dried rose on a table

III

Or they hang like marionettes on nails prattling in
ceaseless synonymic variants first about those

fortunate ones who have not yet lost their ration of
falling then about sports the weather once those

subjects are depleted they resort to animal
husbandry vowel shifts Hegelian dialectics

the statistics of measles thus unwittingly exhausting
the finite number of words assigned to each so that

when they reach the near end of their lexicon they
can be heard repeating the rarefied few words they

never quite had a use for *kimberlite spazierstock
polychondritis viscosity gyot lopolith* some are
overheard muttering *thank you* and *please* and *love*

## Marcellus Shale

When the earth was on fire
the stone god brought her molten mantel
he offered her the pressure of water
he made veins and dikes propagate
through the crust
                        he applied frack jobs
strained the tensile
strength before necking
                        with his hand
he stimulated her wells
                        with his eye
he gauged her permeability

But she cooling made metal
out of gravity

I have them drown in ground-
mass he cried and gravel
I will let siltstone fall
between sandstone and shale
this shall be a lump of Lucifer
this one whose iron oxides still bleed
a fading red shall be Beelzebub
that one whose white vein
of quartz was drawn
like a band by ocean currents
shall be Moloch

Then he asked her to bathe
                in diluvian rains
but she made bones out of water
                and laid them in coal beds

Then he made the bones
fall and fester in vast silent
fractures fathoms deep
miles massed and shattered
broken cleaved layered crushed
toppled over each other or
solitary undefended
on their broadest side

## Of Falling

She after a pause

*The sudden weight has torn them*
                    *down they are*
*not used to being things*


Then to herself

*The river flows and lifts*
*them a little so that they will remember*
                    *their weightlessness they will keep*
*falling until they consist*
*merely of delicate membranes*
*they have to become*
                    *weightless*
*again what they were before*
                    *they were steeped*
*in time and matter*


And he

Each bears the vertigo
caused by its own abyss
                    each falls within
                    its silent radius

(When he had asked her to hold a red breccia
he had felt the lightness of her hand beneath
the stone's weight and far within its solitude
the gaze of ferns and fossils the constancy of
movement and matter)


*Why do I stoop*

                                 *to pick them up?*

*why do I hold them?*
*why when I toss a stone away*
*and its mass and weight stay*

                                 *in the hand for a while*

*and my thoughts are drawn*
*to the place where it might*
*have fallen*
*if I could have found it again*

                                 *so as to find*

*that resonance of a time*
*deeper than ocean and bedrock*


*so as to feel again*


*that each stone exists*
*between time and eternity*
*that all stones are border stones?*

On the last day he takes her finger
and runs it along the stone's side
to let her find the mineral speed
the gravitational constant
she feels the force of matter thrusting
from the stone's blind center
under her hand ripples have formed
on the surface and spread
in rings from the cleft


Let us not have time

                be a movement through space

he says

                but the inwardness of things


*So let this be*
*how a stone*         *falls*
*through the long*

                *shaft of its matter*


*Or does the angel*
*ascend and descend*

*in the innermost compression*
*of the stone's weight?*

When he opens it to find the angel
all he sees in the cleavage
is the laminar flow


(The blossoms of the lavender
have faded the honeysuckle vines
have thickened the evening darkens
and the pit of the window
has the weight of stone)


The house is still
the light brief

then the moon rises
and she knows it will rise

all night and the dark
of the window flows out

it sings and the stones are full
of light their fury abated


*The upheavals of the stone's*
*circumference have slowed*

He feels the movements
of the angel ascending
and descending in the half-

           light of her body


She to herself

*How all things fall*

           *into themselves each in*

*its own slowness*
*because of the void*
*they have brought with them*


He to himself

It is by falling
into the angel that the stone exists

           we too are hosts of angels

we too fall inwardly
the angel opens within us

# Of the Limited Number of Deaths Apportioned to Each

*. . . but I . . . considering the thousand dores that lead*
*to death, doe thank my God that we can die but once.*
SIR THOMAS BROWNE

Although we have long assumed that each of us has
to have only one for some of us it is easy to lay

claim to it several times over by the accident of
birth or by the secret cryptograms of weather work

or war while for others it seems hard to come by it
lingers in wounds and disease and comes a little

at a time but otherwise we think we ought to be
grateful for the single ration of it in proportion to

the unlimited allowance of suffering that is daily
dispensed if we carry our death with us like

an unopened gift if we wait for an anniversary or
the celebration of an appropriate occasion to open

it anxious that it will be the right one since we seem
generally disappointed about its size (it is either too

large or too small) and most want to return it for
another one it is now known that we may have

an allocation of two or three deaths (though some
have as many as dozen and some have only one)

we often recklessly waste the first in a wholly
avoidable accident and then thinking that we

miraculously survived (which is nothing other than
having spent one's first death) live our lives with

utmost prudence or fear only to find out at the end
when we are tired that we have one or two more left

## Of the Disappearance of Size

In these days our bones shine through the body
like elongated fluorescent lamps  and the skin
hangs on it like washed paper these are the signs
                        then they insist they have
seen it all they will stubbornly continue to see us
for a while but without the illusion of grief it is
clear that we disappear every day
                        right before everybody's eyes
one cannot see it not because it always comes too
soon or unexpectedly but because death is tiny as
the sharp tip of a needle we will fit into it our size
has been taken

## The Materialist Dreams of Angels

When in the last century of unceasing wars and
terror the angels lost their wings Titus Lucretius
Carus dreamed that
        angels cannot but assume the physics of
small corpuscles
        their cellular locomotions
        their amoeboid crawlings
        the choreographed arrangements of their
skeletal gliding
        their intracellular transports in the
untraversable centers of stones

all produce nothing but the din of the devouring
underworld

Then in his dream he walked down to the Tiber to
study the certainty of stones
                        their bodies appeared vacant
desolate immobile but Lucretius dreamed they
seemed to lean intimately towards other stones and
he interpreted this leaning
        as the movement of atoms
        as the stones' slow rigid copulations
        as the pleasure of their taut circumferences

When he turned to go back to his house
                        the stones rose out of the river

gray roots with long tubular hairs a phalanx
of things with spears drawn up with shields
overlapping pale children's twelve hundred
winter faces

But to Titus Lucrecius Carus stones were merely
appearances of atomic coagulates uninhabitable
densities their persistence to suffer time to flow in
them at the speed of stone shaped their gray and
speckled solemnities

                a river he thought is merely
the macrocosmic manifestation of a stone's
innermost movement

In his dream's sudden alignments of density and
rarity he saw himself frail as autumn grass
bending down on the shores of the Tiber examining
a stone's swollen nodule

                  he ran his fingers along the
tiny ridge and felt a little tubular opening the span
of spark and heard the stone's slow expiration

                  then he dreamed very
fleetingly (he would not remember it in the
morning) that if angels exist they exist in exact
proportion to a stone's embrace of stone that they
fly by merely leaning towards eternity

(Would he not say in the morning ah looking
at a stone requires practice like walking back into
a room so as to be reminded of what one might have
wanted to remember? that a stone is perhaps
the wingbeat of an angel for when one turns
one's face towards it there is nothing
                              but stone?) but a stone's
revelation might have exactly the length of
forgetting it might reveal itself just as one had
meant to remember


Even in his dream he did not feel them
                         yet he could not doubt that
one does feel a stone's weight and that is (he
concluded) why they *have* weight
                         to make us feel.


He awakened


Looking up at the slack sky hanging over the
terrifying lulls between six wars he thought
in one long breath
                         that we do not know our
holding of the stone determines the direction of the
flow of the embedded crystals in it like flocks of
migrating birds arising centrifugal by the music of
their bodies (while he opened himself)

He was awake that night from mid-moon until dawn
and thought that stones would have kept vigil
with him but only

                he realized if he could have
brushed their sides and gently entered through
the wing clefts or worm voids enough to cause
in the stone the tiniest vibrations of moisture which
in the beginning he knew became the cause
of the unceasing movements of atoms and which
engendered other movements such as the growth
of moss

                or the three Mithridatic wars
then he fell back to dreaming (again) wherein he
briefly despaired

        that stones are depleted wingless on a plain
of clavicles and elongated spines protruding above
the back of wolves like unfeathered blanks

                then he lay in the outlines of
darkness and his life fell on him

                he held the stone in its slow
waking its weight pressing shyly against his palm it
could not be helped it would fall through it and in
this falling no angel would arise

                in the morning he found
crystals in the form of white lenticular foliates
strewn on the stone floor of his chamber and
the wind had ceased

## Of the Limited Amount of Touch
## Apportioned to Each

In the first days before we noticed and started
to protect ourselves in our homes small objects

began to cling to us pebbles leaves little animals
then we heard that some were injured in the streets

by flying pans garden tools nails that collided
with great velocity with any one still out and about

it is now impossible to drive a car or lie in a metal
bed since there is no way to extricate oneself from it

we had hoped this was only a temporary
geomagnetic excursion but it is now clear that it is

a cretaceous superchron of unknown dimensions
we can see cars with drivers magnetized to their

seats crying for help that is no longer available
babies are no longer born only very young children

are able to approach each other to an arm's length
of distance before the two small bodies abruptly

swerve aside and apart each is driven back by
the hand of the one reaching out we are so far

apart that we only conceive of each others' lifted
arms as signs hard to read across the distance

we lean toward each other and stand tilted for
hours our hands outstretched like those of beggars

# Nicodemus Reenters His Mother's Womb

*The position of modern religiosity would hold the "beyond"*
*as no longer being above our heads but in the womb.*
JULIA KRISTEVA


Nicodemus held his palm against his mother's
innermost glandular lining that had begun to
thicken since his reentry
      with the tip of his finger
he found the vascular spaces soon they would
fuse and feed his growing hunger and he could
breathe again meanwhile Nicodemus swam
beneath
      the fountain of his mother's heart
            he lay in the sound of her voice
                he listened to the melody
of her body
      and the music of her speech
even when he slept he felt the rhythm of her gait
            and the wind blew where


it pleased and Nicodemus sensed that his mother
was walking among the palm trees bordering the
River Jordan and he asked himself in the watery
peace of his mother's body what Jesus might
have meant when he said you must be born from
above for Nicodemus doubted the hierarchies of
levels and heights of below and above to
determine the provenance of salvation
            then he wondered if he
could see his mother's face in the endometrium

and he could not but he remembered her face as
the analogue of the womb the face that he saw
when he was born the face that saw him
and that seemed to him then as answering
to his needs as had the amniotic fluids
of the uterine muscle in which he bathed
                              turning his body he rejoiced
in his weightlessness (that is the absence of
sorrow) and his body conveyed a lightness that
would stay with him all his life
                              it is out of this lightness that
he posed the question to Jesus not expecting
to be told to look elsewhere for salvation than
in the music of his mother's heart
            in the cadence of her voice
                        in the swing of her gait
                                    and in the warmth
of her blood


while he fingered in the folds of the mucous
lining his destiny and in the rhythm of her pulse
the length of his life
                              when he was born again his
hearing was more acute he listened less to what
people were saying than to where
                  they placed their breath
                              how they rushed or lingered
in their speaking
                  how they paused among their words
he studied

the movements of their hands
    the tilt of their bodies
        the intonation of their voices
           the cadences of their phrasing
he went and found the disciples sleeping in the
Garden of Gethsemane and Nicodemus lay down in
the murmur of their breath

for angels can only hear the weight of things
their falling
    they move mostly in a cacophony
of sounds of suffering or rarely in the innocent
felicities of laughter music and rhythm
        they confer their presences not on
words for when we speak a great silence
enfolds them

## Of Movements and Signs

All of our movements are signs all
of them are particular to each one
of us each movement of the body
even the way one looks up to check
the time


She holds her hand to her face
she moves her head when she hears
her name called each movement is intimate
a sign of herself and of her singularity
and of each moment in time


Movements of the body are
illegible because they are made
across almost impassable distances
most of them remain unseen like
the swinging of branches or the bending
of lilies under the rain or ash
acorn and oak leaves wafting
in scaled clumps deep
in the current of the river
or the rising of the cold of the earth

If seen they are merely thought of
as the movements of matter (the bending
of flowers the turning of
the hand) many of them are
purposeful and explicable to which
category belong even the intimate
adjustments we make when we cry
and shift slightly in a chair
although each movement (the human
gait being the most singular) if decipherable
would be utterly revealing


Someone in the distance would
raise an arm to answer and we
would turn our faces and lift our
hands in response to the sign
of the arm and these would be
interstices openings
each to the other


The abrasions of grief in
the tissues that had turned into cysts
and inflammations hard to
the touch would have been lifted like
the lids on boxes swelled in storage

and the thread root of breath
would have been white
and exposed


She turns her hand reaching up to
seize something she hears voices
someone carries a cup across
a room to a sick child the child
sits up in the graying light slowly
lifting a hand towards the cup


And all is still for a moment
and there are voices across
the distance and signs


Time is a void to leap across she
calculates the hours until she can
go to sleep like a jumper who
needs a certain distance to gain
her speed and turns to face
the distance she looks up
she holds out her hand

## Rose Shouldered the Feather

A man sat bent over the beginning of the wind
he held a feather against it it had not yet moved
he waited for the wind then his feather nodded

and the wind flew out and the man poured
the wind into a bottle then he rose shouldered
his feather and the wind in the bottle and walked

to the stones and brushed them with his feather
gentle as light and the stones awakened and
the man heaved them into a bag rose shouldered

the feather the wind in the bottle the stones in
the bag and went to darkness he slid the feather
into the darkness and held it there long and

still as stone when he withdrew it the light
slipped out through the feather's slit in the
darkness and the man put the light into a purse

rose shouldered the feather the wind in the bottle
the stones in the bag and the light in the purse
then he stepped to the shores of a long river

and waved the feather over the water in the
rhythm of the great blue heron's step and the river
stopped and he lifted it out of its bed and rolled it

up in the wind and tied it with light and rose
shouldered the feather the wind in the bottle
the stones in the bag the light in the purse

the river rolled up in the wind tied with light
and the man carried the wind the stones the light
and the river and said to whomever he met

let me cool you with my wind rest your head on
my stones see my light drink of my river here is
my feather dip it into a heart and someone dipped

it rose shouldered the feather the wind in the bottle
the stones in the bag the light in the purse the river
rolled up in the wind and tied with light

# On Being Told to Be Cheerful

*La terre est bleu comme une orange*
PAUL ÉLUARD

I was blue.  I cried, "I'm dancing on the lovely
orange sun!"  But orange was blue to me.  Then
the sun came through the blue cry, and I danced
and sang to the beat of my feet, and the blue stuck
to the lovely orange until the sun was blue under my
feet.  My feet, blue from crying, had dyed the sun's
golden orange to a cold blue hue, "very ugly,"
I said, "too blue!" And I kneeled on my knees and
stooped very low on the ugly blue sun and tucked
my feet under my seat like a saint, "so that my blue
feet won't taint the lovely orange sun," I said, and
kneeled down on the blue sun and cried softly into
my feet and prayed that the sun would turn lovely
and orange again, but oh it was blue, it was blue.

## The Sum of All Suffering Is Constant

The distribution of suffering is based on
the availability of hosts their ages genders

certain climate conditions race history
although it seems rationed fitfully and mostly

to the poor the sum of all suffering is constant
if you are well it is because someone else

has your disease on the day when someone
needs your health a fever is transferred into

you from a distant room reeking of stale
breath there someone despite doctors' predictions

rises and walks into the light while you take
your turn to lie down to be ill for as long

as it takes to find a suitable recipient for
your disease and if no one can be found

you will die and if one can be found
but will be too weak to bear your disease

and dies then his suffering will rise from
his body leap like fire until someone walks

through it despite doctors' predictions while
you rise he lies down in the fire of his body

# Winter

The fields for hundreds of years fields of grass
potatoes sugar beets or wheat are a graveyard
where the stones stand steeply northward
and the country road is a suburban street
here my father lies dead by his own hand
on Saint Nicholas day in his apartment five
floors up here my mother followed him two
months later in the same winter the weather
wears the bones in the body down to the heart

# Elegy for a Suicide

E. S.

(1925–1985)

*The children waited for the wonderworker.*
*Instead of putting coins in their shoes*
*He made a red rose bloom in December.*

JINDRÎSKÂ NIKOLAOSOVÁ

The night does not fall here it descends in a rhythm
of solar obliqueness the river clamors and mutters
into beddings of silt flotsam wars drowned children
spit on the rims of bowls
        I feel the draft like a funnel of wind
five stories below everything has been drawn into it
stumps an upper jaw a stream of mucus bandages
when the sandbanks break I let myself drift in
the undertow the pits and sudden caves I wade
across stagnant pools where the water lies stinking
dark under a film of sludge thick with pollen
        even from the height of bridges and
windows even on this tipping shelf of France among
stones and high sycamores whose winged fruits
flutter through the air whose leaves have turned
and fallen seven times since I last leaned out
toward them

The river subsides the sandbanks lengthen boats
lie tilted on the riverbed the summer solstice

has passed a man walks his dog on the Quai du
Pont Neuf
                    though I still have to bring each day
to its end in this long northern twilight I have
entered the estuary of your life
                    no one had seen you hiding from your
death while you made your Sunday visits later each
of your phone calls even silences assumed proleptic
resonance that day early in December when you
took off your coat and the sudden exertion of your
arms like a swimmer's reaching for the shore broke
your tears


Your arms had been full of breaking that night on
St. Nicholas day you held your hands up cried them
dipped them into your body stirred them whipped
them white as embers
                    in the body's glass each hand had
a bone light pressed out of it the body broke the
hands slid down the length of it grasping it if
they could have grasped lifting it if it could have
been lifted


The landscape opens to fields of wheat and corn
wisps of poppies and cosmos flower by the road
                    I wait for you in the rhythm of light
I assume the pace of water I lean in the shadow of

stone under this open window a listener of the river
a hearer of the broken light of water
                    last night I woke and felt the crossing
of our ages like the waft of someone passing closely
in the dark I wonder at what moment I first
survived you to salvage the cast of your eyes your
furtive smile the fragile economy of your gestures


The sycamores are shedding long curved fragments
of bark onto the promenade
                    each leaf each shimmer of light on
the water proclaims its small material destiny
                    the wheat has been harvested
the grapes ripen on the vine the nights lengthen
the river scours its caustic bed of lime
                    we sleep in unhurried destinations
in the trembling air over distant fields far beyond
the steep slate roofs of Touraine the Loire flows
in a tranquil pitch toward the Atlantic seacoast
                    releasing you to gather pinecones
in the bohemian winter

## But Do Not Let Them Know You Were Alone When You Died

Leave it behind it will be too cumbersome to bear
across the vast fields it only lengthens the distance
of dying but do not let them think you were alone
when you died
                    speak early of your grief
to someone you loved and of your love earlier
to someone you lost do not take love with you leave
it with them leave without it so as not to leave
with sorrow too let neither love nor sorrow nor
grief hinder the awkward coming undone let it
not make you miss
                    your step already swathed
in shrouds of blindness let it go let them wonder
how light you have become in the quiet raft
of your body
                    and do not let them know you
were alone when you died look they are waiting
for you by the river

# In Gratitude for the Slowness of Granite

Though some lie open where they cleft
in the sheered breaches hewn by ages
and a small amount of fire that had been
enclosed since the beginning of time
still flutes into the air in the form of glitter
and residual noises from earliest cataclysms
still ooze through pores in little sighs
from where a granite's underside settles
into the mud's yielding like a rough pit
into fruit's flesh

                  God thank you if the granites'
cooling their igneous noises their breaking
their solitude were to happen in a human
lifespan it would be unbearable so that in
their slowness we live and are briefly saved

## And If a Day Is Left to Me Before I'm Old

And if a day is left to me before I'm old I will go
past the bridge through the barren snow-covered
field along the curved lines of the cut corn stalks
standing like thrown sticks and beyond the field
down the slight fernslept incline where the river's
slab of skylight glides stately down the seasons

And I will go to the river if a day is left to me
before I'm old for there the wind-tubes play
strange music "go to Circe by the river go to get
her haul the swine out of you like a sack of pain"

And I go and I bend over a fold of wind to hear myself
missing if I didn't go missing before and I'm old and
I think of my ashes falling like sleep from a bridge
and your sorrow wading across a bed of river stones

## Little Fugue
(Postscript)


I weighed the wind in scales made of the flight
of birds I weighed the flight of birds in scales

made of glass I measured the circumference
of the light in the glass with a compass made of

transparency I weighed the light in the scales
of the silences between women and men and

the silences in scales made of words and I used
the remainder of a silence to find happiness or

bitterness I found happiness and I weighed it
in scales made of lost time then I weighed lost

time in scales made of hands cupped to hold water
I walked to the end of a long river to weigh

the river in scales made of water I weighed it
by holding it up to a window and its light and

I weighed the light and measured
the circumference of the light in the glass
with a compass made of transparency

# Notes

"Of Angels"
This poem's epigraph from Rainer Maria Rilke,
". . . *es nähme / einer mich plötzlich ans Herz . . . ,*"
can be translated as ". . . if one of them suddenly /
pressed me to his heart . . ."

"Antoine Le Sauteur, Maître de Cave"
This poem's epigraph is from an obituary that
appeared in the French newspaper *Le Dauphiné libéré.*
The musical notations are by Molly Rose Brown.

"On Being Told to Be Cheerful"
This poem's epigraph from **Paul Éluard**, "*La terre est
bleu comme une orange,*" can be translated as "The
world is blue like an orange."

# Acknowledgments

I thank Katie Ford for her angelic interventions, G. C. Waldrep for his astute aesthetic judgment, and Tess Gallagher for her abiding support. I also thank my friends and colleagues Charles Borkhuis, Molly Rose Brown (who did the musical notations for "Antoine Le Sauteur, Maître de Cave"), Kathy Graham, Katie Hays, Pete Mackey, Shara McCallum, Mardi Mumford, Kathleen Page, Jim Rice, and Gary Steiner for their kind responses to my poems, and Pauline and David Fletcher for their benevolence during a difficult time. My editors at Tupelo Press, Jeffrey Levine and Jim Schley, have been wonderfully encouraging. I am deeply grateful to my wife, Saundra Kay Morris, first confidant of my secret writings, always my first reader and most discerning editor, always unfailingly supportive. Thank you all from my heart.

I also thank the editors of the following publications where these poems, some in different versions, first appeared:

*The American Poetry Review*, "Of Stones and Angels"

*The Cincinnati Review*, "Of Angels"

*Diode*, "The Disappearance of Size," "Little Fugue" and "Of the Limited Amount of Touch Apportioned to Each," "Of the Limited Number of Deaths Apportioned to Each"

*The Kenyon Review*, "But Do Not Let Them Know You Were Alone When You Died"

*Narrative*, "Antoine Le Sauteur, Maître de Cave" and "Nicodemus Reenters His Mother's Womb"

*The New Orleans Review*, "Of Movements and Signs"

*Pleiades*, "Of the Limited Amount of Hatred Apportioned to Each," "Of the Limited Amount of Falling Apportioned to Each," and "Of the Limited Amount of Silence Light and Space"

*Ploughshares*, "Winter"

*Poetry International*, "The Materialist Dreams of Angels"

"Of Falling" appeared as a mixed-genre piece in the book *Crrritic: Critical Inventions*, edited by J. Schad and O. Tearle (Sussex Academic Press, 2011).

## Other books from Tupelo Press

See our complete list at www.tupelopress.org

CPSIA information can be obtained at www.ICGtesting.com
Printed in the USA
BVOW02s0349190615

404505BV00001B/2/P

9 781936 797639